Social Work Day

International Congress of Qualitative Inquiry

*Theme: Qualitative Inquiry
& the Politics of Resistance*

Official Program

Illini Union
University of Illinois
Urbana, Illinois, USA
Thursday, 16 May 2019

Social Work Day is the great qualitative social work get-together. Held each May at the International Congress of Qualitative Inquiry (ICQI) in Urbana, IL, USA, Social Work Day attracts researchers from throughout the world. This is the premier international qualitative social work conference where scholars present cutting edge research using both traditional and innovative qualitative methods of qualitative inquiry.

Norman Denzin is the director of ICQI, Dr. Denzin is emeritus Distinguished Professor of Communications, College of Communications Scholar, and Research Professor of Communications, Sociology, and Humanities, University of Illinois, Urbana-Champaign, USA.

Jane Gilgun is the organizer of Social Work Day. Dr. Gilgun is professor, School of Social Work, University of Minnesota, Twin Cities, USA.

Many thanks to Austin Oswald, Graduate Center of the City University of New York, who helped organize this program.

The papers are organized into panels based primarily on methods and methodologies.

Cover Photo by Jane Gilgun: Kathy Charmaz, ICQI 2018, recipient of Lifetime Achievement Award

ISBN: 9781097296965
Imprint: Independently published

Social Work Day
Thursday, 16 May 2019

Theme: Qualitative Inquiry and the Politics of Resistance
Jane F. Gilgun, University of Minnesota, Twin Cities, Organizer

8-8:30

Welcome & Introductions   Union Illini Room A

8:30-9:20

Opening Plenary Roundtable:
Qualitative Social Work as Resistance

Chair: Jane F. Gilgun, University of Minnesota, Chair
Union Illini Room A

Qualitative social work is resistance. Panel members will do brief presentations on how their qualitative inquiry complicates and challenges grand narratives and power structures. The stories and experiences of research participants are counter-stories that raise awareness and lead to social change. Members of the audience will join in a discussion of how their qualitative inquiry is resistance. Qualitative social work's claim to be resistive is rooted in its history in British settlement houses, Booth's in-depth research, LePlay's ethnographies of European workers, the emancipatory philosophy of Simmel, Dilthey, and pragmatist philosophies, and U.S. settlements, particularly Hull House in Chicago.

Neha Rajiv Deshmukh, Columbia University
Magnus Mfoafo-M'Carthy, Wilfrid Laurier University
Tracie Rogers, University of the Southern Caribbean
Rita Sørly, Norut Northern Research Institute

9:30-10:50
Concurrent Sessions

Critical Theories 1: Race and Gender
Chair: Sarah Jen, University of Kansas
Union 314A

1526849 **Visualizing Multiracial Identity Development: Participatory Diagramming as Visual Expression of Multiracial Experiences.** *Sarah Yang Mumma (smumma@smith.edu) Smith College and Kelly F. Jackson (kelly.f.jackson@asu.edu) Arizona State University*

As the U.S. becomes increasingly diverse there is a growing need to understand the significance of culture, race, and ethnicity on identity development.

3

Unfortunately, existing research on ethnic identity development habitually disregards the growing population of multiracial persons, or persons who identify with two or more racial groups and resist being partialized into historic single race categories. This significantly constrains our ability to disentangle some of the presumed links between ethnic identity development, risk, resilience, and psychological functioning among one of the fastest growing racial groups in the US. Utilizing a critical multiracial theory (MultiCrit) framework and visual grounded theory to analyze 25 participatory diagrams, or visual timelines created by multiracial study participants, this study contributes new insights into the contextually rich and dynamic processes comprising multiracial identity development and seeks to disrupt dominant discourses regarding multiracial identities and experiences.

1490791 **Breaking Through the Whiteness?: A Critical Race Examination of Secondary Educator Perceptions of School Discipline.** *Michael Massey (masseym@vcu.edu) Virginia Commonwealth University*

Working with semi-structured interviews of educators at one high school, I conducted a hybrid deductive and inductive thematic analysis to examine educator perceptions of school discipline, racial disproportionality in discipline, and the implementation of a new disciplinary framework, Schoolwide Positive Behavior Interventions and Supports (SWPBIS). Using a critical race theory analytical lens to center issues of race and racism, the interviews revealed a school that is deeply structured to maintain and valorize whiteness. While many of the educators were concerned about racial disparities and able to identify systemic barriers to achieving equity, they simultaneously relied on discursive strategies that reinforced racial stratification and upheld whiteness. This paper will discuss the findings, highlight the utility of qualitative, critical race approaches to education and social work research, and consider points of collaboration between social work and education to advance social justice.

1490419 **Choosing Family, Queering Kinship: A Conceptual Inquiry of "Chosen Family" for a Contemporary Context.** *Nina Jackson Levin* (ninalev@umich.edu*) University of Michigan, Erica Watson, University of Michigan, Emily Piellusch, University of Michigan, and Shanna K. Kattari (skattari@umich.edu) University of Michigan*

"Chosen family" is a signature of the queer experience. So why does choosing family become an act of queering kinship? This paper addresses the stakes of chosen family if formed besides or beyond living as queer. There are many reasons individuals choose to form communities that serve as families, particularly in a neoliberal environment that prioritizes free movement and individualization. Yet chosen family is a refuge specifically generated by and for the queer experience. Is it possible to make chosen families amongst non-queer communities without coopting the power and submerging the history of the term? This paper explores such questions by tracing the limits and possibilities of "family" across three domains: social, legal, medical. Drawing from kinship, queer, and feminist theories, this article interrogates the liminality staked at the boundary of community and family in an attempt to define and nuance both terms for a contemporary context.

1483965 **Discourses of Bisexuality Among Older Women.** *Sarah Jen (srjen@ku.edu) University of Kansas*

Historical and discursive context are largely unexamined factors in shaping the lived experience of bisexuality and aging. This study applied critical feminist and life course perspectives to explore how older bisexual women (N=12) construct their bisexual identities and subjectivity in in-depth interviews. Findings of a Foucualdian Discourse Analysis reveal two divergent groups of women, the Early Emergers and Mature Migrators, who differ in their constructions of bisexuality and the timing of their first experienced attractions to other women. While the Early Emergers construct bisexuality as a stable, biological concept, the Mature Migrators challenge this narrative by emphasizing the fluidity of sexuality through discourses of migration spurred by "light bulb" moments. Scholars and practitioners must intentionally critique and contribute to discourses of bisexuality and theoretically, added attention to fluidity, life course patterns, and historical context can offer a better understanding of discursive constructions and the lived experience of sexuality.

What is Social Work Knowledge and What Do We Do With It?
Chair: *James Drisko, Smith Colleg*
Union 314B

1490479 **Decolonizing Social Work Research.** *Austin Oswald (aoswald@gradcenter.cuny.edu) Graduate Center of the City University of New York*

Over the past few decades, social work has enhanced its research profile by adopting a particular dialect of scientific evidence, rooted in physics envy, that views randomized control trials and evidence-based practice as the gold standard of social work research and practice. Indeed, this shift in research has permeated doctoral education and research training. Little attention, however, has been given to pedagogical approaches to train doctoral students into an epistemology of social work, and the impact of hegemonic discourses on their understanding of evidence and scientific inquiry. This autoethnographic study weaves together personal narratives with institutional discourses to understand how this disciplining of my body, relationships, and versions of science interfere with my social justice commitments to social work research. The study traces back to the origins of social work to glean insights into how doctoral students can resist and expand prevailing research hierarchies to include critical qualitative methodologies.

1518417 **Knowledge Translation in the Knowledge-Based Economy: Expanding or Reducing the Field of Current Research?** *Gabriela Novotna (gabriela.novotna@uregina.ca) University of Regina*

Health researchers in Canada have undertaken new roles and responsibilities constructed by the notion of "knowledge translation" (KT) hailed as offering a great promise for narrowing the research-practice gap. Accordingly, evidence-based practice (EBP) has become the desired result of successfully closing the gap between knowledge creation and its application. Despite the perception of KT and EBP as necessary, beneficial, and universal, both concepts are rarely critically examined as the tools for the governance of health research. In this presentation, we will address the importance of conceptualizing knowledge in the "knowledge translation" metaphor as "created," "collectively negotiated" but also "competitive" and "elitist." Furthermore, we will challenge complacency with the understanding of KT as being neutral and representing a "good thing" and critically analyze the co-product of knowledge translation -- an "evidence-based" movement -- and its potential for being a tool for promoting neo-liberal agenda.

1490550 **On Generalization in Qualitative Research.** *James Drisko (jdrisko@smith.edu) Smith College*

Qualitative research is often challenged for a lack of generalizability. Are qualitative research findings really so limited? Generalization is the creation of concepts from specific instances by abstracting important common properties. However, verification of the fit research-based concepts to other settings, actions and epistemologies is always required: No approach to generalization guarantees applicability to other settings, persons or times. Still, qualitative research findings do provide concepts and evidence that can guide thinking applicable to other persons and situations.

This paper explores how qualitative methodologists conceptualize generalization. Views examined include Blumer's sensitizing concepts, Guba and Lincoln's nomothetic generalization, Firestone's analytic generalization, Campbell's proximal similarity case to case generalizability), and Therart's argumentative generalization. Not all qualitative research seeks to support generalization, but it surely can! Thick description, holism, immersion in data, self-reflection, reflexivity and the integration of evidence may maximize the potential for generalization or transferability of qualitative research findings and concepts.

1490561 **A (Brief) Introduction to Meta-Ethnography: The Pioneering Qualitative Meta-Synthesis Methodology** *James Drisko (jdrisko@smith.edu) Smith College*

Meta-ethnography [ME] is the first, and most often employed, method of synthesizing multiple qualitative research reports. Created by Noblit and Hare (1988), ME detailed the seven steps of the full synthesis process, and both identified and examined several pros and cons of synthesizing multiple studies. These seven steps were widely used in other, later, qualitative and quantitative synthesis approaches. This paper will provide an overview of the ME process. An interpretive method, ME seeks to maintain an emic understanding of data, concepts, and explanatory frameworks through an iterative, inductive process.

Challenges regarding epistemological variation, locating qualitative publications, sampling, setting inclusion criteria and data analysis are each examined. ME's core analytic techniques a) reciprocal translation, b) refutational analysis, and c) lines of argument synthesis are described and differentiated. Several published examples of ME are identified in an extensive print handout. France et al.'s protocol for ME quality assessment is also introduced.

Understanding Violence Through Qualitative Methods
Chair: Kyee Altranice Young (kyoun10@louisville.edu) University of Louisville
Union 404

1489783 **Wrestling with Positionality and Advocacy: Clarification through Collaboration.** *Taylor J Ellis (tjellis1@crimson.ua.edu) University of Alabama and Megan Sawyer (masawyer16@gmail.com) University of Alabama*

CEO Fighting Game Championships and New Japan Pro Wrestling hosted an event in Daytona Beach, Florida in order to "give the Fighting Game Community and East Coast Wrestling fans a taste of NJPW's high intensity action this summer with a live wrestling show." At this event, there was an unannounced dark match between two local talents, Chasyn Rance and Aaron Epic. This probably would have been no issue had Rance not been a registered sex offender.

Finding myself in the role of researcher, advocate, and professional wrestling fan, I felt the need to respond. I wrote a response to the backlash, but before submitting my response article, I consulted with a colleagues who serves youth with problematic sexual behaviors. Through discussion, I realized my positionality was absent from the article, which impeded my ability to empower individuals with sexual behavior problems and educate others.

1520824 **"Not no is not yes:" Ambiguity, Temporality, and Agency as Concepts Influencing and Confounding Consent in College Student Hookup Relationships.** *Melissa Hardesty (hardesty@binghamton.edu), Sarah Reta Young (syoung@binghamton.edu), Sean Massey (smassey@binghamton.edu), Ann Merriwether (amerriwe@binghamton.edu), and Maggie Parker (mparke11@binghamton.edu)*

Affirmative consent, a conceptual and linguistic reframing of what constitutes permissible and morally acceptable sexual activity, is increasingly popular on college campuses across the United States. Lauded by some as a tool to combat rape culture (Aliment, 2015), affirmative consent has also been described by critics as unwieldy and out-of-synch with normative sexual practices (Bennett, 2016). This focus group study (n=33) asks how college students understand and navigate consent in their casual sexual encounters, and how these practices square with their university's affirmative consent policy. Open and thematic coding revealed three interrelated themes consistent with symbolic interactionism (Goffman, 1959): ambiguity, temporality, and agency. Participants reported that sexual interest is usually communicated indirectly through para-verbal gestures and body language; direct verbal communication usually occurs in the form of "checking in" after sexual activity has begun; and descriptions of normative sexual encounters frequently feature missing, passive, or compromised sexual agents.

1520264 The Qualitative Component in a Multi-Stage, Mixed-Methods Comparative Case Study Examining Parental Perceptions of Sibling Violence. *Nathan H. Perkins (nperkins2@luc.edu) Loyola University Chicago*

This presentation highlights the qualitative component of a mixed methods comparative case study project that examined parental perceptions and experiences of physical and emotional sibling violence. Using a case study methodology (Yin,2014), I will discuss the collection and analysis of data provided by seven parents in a three-phase data collection process to ascertain differences and similarities to how participants perceived physical and emotional sibling violence and sibling rivalry. I will show the benefits of using matrices (Miles & Huberman, 1994) to allow for presenting similarities and differences among participant responses from four different family structures. Finally, I will discuss lessons learned from engaging in a multi-stage data collection and data analytic process including the consideration of time, participant reflection, and triangulation.

1525964 Are we woke?" Exploring the Development and Impact of Critical Consciousness (CC) Development Within a Youth Violence Prevention Program. *Kyee Altranice Young (kyoun10@louisville.edu) University of Louisville and Monique Ingram Williams (monique.ingram@louisville.edu) University of Louisville*

This study explores the critical consciousness (cc) development process and its consequences for urban minority youth at a Center for Disease Control and Prevention National Center of Excellence in Youth Violence Prevention (YVPC). A case study approach was used to conduct in-depth interviews with 12 youth matriculating through a fellowship within the YVPC. Grounded theory techniques were used for data analysis. Youth display varying levels of understanding related to their cc development processes; and thus, exhibit an array of reactionary emotions in relation to their changing personal paradigm. A process model was developed to explicate the development and progression of cc and praxis within these participants. I will present recommendations for engaging youth in critical consciousness development and discuss why it should be central in programs that engage marginalized minority youth.

Social Work Education
Chair: *Ben Miller, University of Louisville*
Union 405

1489780 Giving Students the Opportunity to Engage in Activism and Discourse through the Unity Wall Project. *Taylor J Ellis (tjellis1@crimson.ua.edu), Kimberly Gibson (kgibson2@crimson.ua.edu) University of*

Alabama, Nicole Ruggiano (nruggiano@ua.edu) University of Alabama, and Alexis Ferruccio (aferruccio@law.gwu.edu) George Washington University Law School

An ongoing challenge for social work educators is how best to engage students in activities that promote social justice (Adams, 2004; Droppa 2007). Yet, teaching social work students to respond to societal injustices is demanded by our code of ethics and professional values (NASW, 2008). As a response to shootings and other violent activities reflecting homophobia and racism in 2016 and the divisive nature of the presidential election, social work field faculty facilitated student social justice activities, which led to the creation of the Unity Wall. The Unity Wall involved a partnership and hands-on advocacy activities with the campus police department. Boards were set up in the campus student center where approximately 400 students participated in expressing their Hopes and Fears about society, the political climate, police and community relations, and their own futures. An informal forum with local law enforcement to discuss the responses followed the event.

1525989 **Researching Expert Decision Making: Using Applied Cognitive Task Analysis (ACTA) to Study Expert Lobbyist Practices--and Beyond!** *Joseph D. Minarik (jminarik@illinois.edu) University of Illinois*

Social work educators are often in a position of training students to develop real-world practice skills. The decision making models offered to students can be limited, however. For instance, in the area of lobbying, various sources of lobbyist practices exist which are based on individual lobbyist experiences over time. Those stories are important, but might reflect circumstances and factors unique to that individual. Such a limitation can be overcome by studies which use within- and cross-case comparison. The Applied Cognitive Task Analysis (ACTA) approach, used extensively by Department of Defense instructional designers, is an ideal qualitative method for investigating expert decision making in the real world. This paper illustrates the use of ACTA to investigate how and why expert state lobbyists share information with legislators. The paper also illustrates how knowledge generated by such studies can be applied to curriculum development, training, and instructional design.

1522756 **Students with Visual Impairments in Higher Education in Vietnam: Faculty Awareness on Providing Accommodations.** *Thi Thanh Tuyen Bui (ttbui2@illinois.edu) University of Illinois*

As the workforce increasingly requires skilled employees, more youths attend a post-secondary school and so do youths with visual impairments. For visually impaired students, accommodations significantly affect their educational trajectories in higher education. This study explores faculty awareness of providing accommodations for visually impaired students in Vietnam from both students' and faculty's perspectives. This multiple case-based study drew on in-depth interviews with 20 visually impaired students on their experiences with accommodations they received on campus. I also interviewed three faculty members on their experiences in lecturing visually impaired students. Thematic-style analyses were undertaken to identify emerging themes and meaning units. Visually impaired students perceived the accommodations provided by colleges as inadequate and faculty did not have positive attitudes in assisting them. This study's findings imply that raising faculty awareness on disability is the key point to improve providing accommodations for visually impaired and students with disabilities in Vietnam.

1490618 A Phenomenological Study of Compassion Satisfaction Among Social Work Educators. *Ben Miller (ben.miller@louisville.edu) University of Louisville, Sultan Ali Shubair (salshubair@siu.edu) University of Louisville, and Jean Zelenko (jean.zelenko@louisville.edu) University of Louisville*

Compassion satisfaction is a popular phenomenon being studied among the helping professions. We identified a gap in the literature when we found no studies that focused on compassion satisfaction among social work educators. This study seeks to explore how this population defines and sustains compassion satisfaction. We conducted in-depth interviews with 20 social work educators and used constructivist grounded theory techniques for the analysis. We found that experiences of compassion satisfaction differed among participants. Some equated compassion satisfaction with great classroom conversations, while others associated it with role modeling for students. Similarly, all referred to issues of work-life balance and self-care as measures to sustain it. We will present recommendations for identifying and sustaining compassion satisfaction.

11:00-12:20
Concurrent Sessions

Critical Theories 2: Critical Discourse Analysis
Jessica Lee (jel6@iu.edu) *Indiana University*
Union 314A

1489321 Interrogating the Construction of Criminalized Women in the Social Work Literature: A Critical Discourse Analysis. *Sandra M Leotti (sleotti@pdx.edu) Portland State University*

Drawing on findings from a Foucauldian inspired critical discourse analysis, this paper examines the hegemonic ways in which social work engages with criminalized women. Results indicate that social work privileges a psychological discourse and that the assessment and management of risk has supplanted a holistic approach to meeting client needs. I argue that social work's growing dedication to practices that seek to adjust the psychological fortitude of individuals relies on wider cultural discourses of responsibilization, which reproduce, rather than interrupt criminalization, and divert attention away from the need for broader social and economic change. This, I conclude, reflects a neo-liberal political climate and aligns social work with penal institutions in troubling ways. This analysis exposes how social work is implicated in processes of criminalization and propels a shift in emphasis from individualized service delivery, aimed at changing the behavior of individuals, to launching interventions that tackle structural injustice and inequity

1525939 **Voice and Inclusion in Research with Women with Histories of Substance Use and Incarceration.** *Alana Gunn (agunn2@uic.edu) University of Illinois at Chicago and Melissa Hardesty (hardesty@binghamton.edu) Binghamton University*

Ethics specific research efforts have provided evidence of the risks and benefits of engaging vulnerable populations in research. Formerly incarcerated women with drug histories represent a vulnerable population due to their past trauma and the gendered stigmas attached to their experiences with imprisonment and drug use. Considering the implications for harm, this study explores the research experiences of 28 formerly incarcerated women. Content-based thematic analysis was used to identify common conceptualizations among the participants' narratives. Study findings revealed benefits to participation such as raising awareness through disclosure, as well as the need for women to share their experiences to promote their personal healing and recovery. Participants also reported risks such as emotional distress through the reliving of trauma and fears regarding researcher stigma. Findings speak to the implications for more trauma-informed interviewing practices that consider the role of the researcher, the research environment, and how they contribute to one's recovery.

Human Rights and Changing Refugee Resettlement Policies: A Critical Discourse Analysis. *Jessica Lee* (jel6@iu.edu) Indiana University

This paper will provide a comparative discussion of refugee resettlement policies among the 37 countries that participate in the UN Refugee Agency's resettlement program. Using critical discourse analysis and a human rights framework, the presenters will discuss changing refugee policies and analyze the human rights implications. The 1951 Convention relating to the status of refugees and the 1967 Protocol outline the legal concept of the "refugee" (UNHCR, 2018). Presently, policy changes and nationalist sentiments worldwide are polemical. This forced discussion will examine the construction of forced migration by posing the question, "who is a refugee?" Due to policy changes since 2016, US refugee arrival numbers has sharply declined. The presenters will connect this to other migrant groups in the US such as Deferred Action for Childhood Arrivals recipients and undocumented migrant families. This presentation will carry implications for global social work practice with refugees and migrants.

Structural Oppressions and Vulnerabilities:
Bringing Stories to the Forefront to Change Policies and Practice
Chair: *Debra Nelson-Gardell, University of Alabama*
Union 314B

1510232 **Indigenous Mothering in the Context of Child Welfare: Stories of Resilience, Resistance, and Resurgence.** *Natalie St-Denis (nstdeni@ucalgary.ca) University of Calgary, Janis Lyn Favel (jlfavel@hotmail.com) Kawacatoose Cree Nation, Joanna Marie Moore (jobean27@hotmail.com) Nigigoonsiminikaaning First Nation, and Christine Ann Walsh (cwalsh@ucalgary.ca) University of Calgary.*

The profession of social work has a historical and ongoing role in the oppression of Indigenous Peoples, in particular, practices by Canada's child welfare system which continue to take a disproportionate number of Indigenous children away from their mothers, families and communities. This modern day "humanitarian crisis" echoes the devastating assimilationist tactics of the residential school system and the 60s scoop, which is a term used to describe Canada's practice of separating Indigenous children and families. As a result, Indigenous mothers continue to be forcibly deprived of their roles and responsibilities of mothering, and Indigenous children are deprived of love, kinship and culture. This paper brings together voices of Indigenous mothers who share their stories of resilience, resistance and resurgence in the face of child welfare systems. These stories challenge current child welfare practices and recommend alternative perspectives for supporting Indigenous mothers and their families

1521371 **"How I long to be married:" Narratives of Single Mothers.** *Tumani Malinga alingat@mopipi.ub.bw) University of Botswana*

Low-income women are amongst the vulnerable groups and continue to live in poverty, and face intimate partner violence. Challenges they face point to the need to address and reduce women's vulnerabilities. A narrative approach was conducted with fifteen low-income single Botswana mothers. Thematic analysis indicated that some women belief marriage can be a breakthrough from struggles. They further stated singlehood as contributing to the difficulties and frustration they have. They narrated how they wished for marriage proposal. The frustration of singlehood was borne due to the stigma attached to being single and being perceived as not woman enough in the community. A few other women however had a different perspective to marriage. The results indicate the need for women to be educated and empowered to be aware that life challenges can be addressed without a man. Programs need to focus on empowering women to be self-sustaining

1490415 **From Resistance to Commitment: Challenges and "Dialectical Milestones" in Creating Research Partnerships in the Child Welfare System.** *Tali Topilsky-Bayer (TaliT@jdc.org) JDC-Brookdale Institute, Guy Enosh (enosh@research.haifa.ac.il) University of Haifa, Aya Almog (AyaAl@jdc.org) JDC-Brookdale Institute, and Hani Nouman (hnouman@univ.haifa.ac.il) University of Haifa.*

The goal of this presentation is to demonstrate a dialectical model for coping with research noncompliance at the child-welfare system. A dialectical approach maintains that an array of milestones can be defined between resistance and full cooperation of research partners. Paradoxically, as some of these milestones are perceived as obstacles to knowledge attainment, they may actually catalyze improved knowledge construction. We adopt a reflective perspective, examining a research project that observed professional decision making in fifty statutorily committees, at the child protection system. The project, which required high levels of partners' involvement, originated with noncompliance and antagonistic attitudes of stakeholders and participants. Through this illustration and voices of research partners, we will present: a) milestones in the researcher–partner relationship; b) contributions of these milestones to knowledge constructing in this project; c) a dialectical model for enhancing research alliances and knowledge construction at the child welfare system

1489785 Feedback Session: Unheard Stories From Middle Eastern Immigrant Female IPV Survivors: A Qualitative Study. *Burcu Ozturk (bozturk@crimson.ua.edu) University of Alabama and Debra Nelson-Gardell (dnelsong@sw.ua.edu) University of Alabama*

In this session, we seek feedback on a dissertation research project that is in progress. Globally, 35% of women have experienced either physical and/or sexual intimate partner violence or non-partner sexual violence (WHO, 2013). Although IPV influences individuals from all racial backgrounds,socio-economic statuses and geographic locations, some communities are more vulnerable, such as immigrants in the U.S.(Hass, Dutton & Orloff, 2000). The purpose of this phenomenological study is to understand the lived experiences and first-hand accounts of Middle Eastern-born immigrant women in the United States, as well as how culture influences these experiences. In addition, the study will explore women's coping mechanisms in diverse cultural contexts to help professionals understand women's survival strategies. The study relies on semi-structured interviews and a plan to recruit approximately ten Middle Eastern immigrant women for the study interviews. Following a short overview of the study methods, the presentation's aim concerns garnering presentation participants' input into the research process, depending on the stage at which the research stands at the time of the ICQI conference.

Grounded Theory and Deductive Methods--Together at Last: Workshop on Retroduction
Chair: Jane Gilgun, University of Minnesota
Union 404

The purpose of this workshop is to show how qualitative social work researchers can use both inductive and deductive approaches in their inquiries. Pierce (1969) called this approach *retroduction*. Retroductive logic provides a rationale for the use of initial conceptual material that focuses the inquiry by providing sensitizing concepts and often ideas (hypotheses) to test, revise, and possibly refute. This is the deductive aspect of retroduction. Induction becomes part of the inquiry in at least two ways: when researchers seek material that 1) they hope will falsify and elaborate upon the initial material and 2) they observe phenomena that their prior material did not anticipate. Researchers may be temporarily flummoxed until they find concepts and theories that appear to fit the phenomena they observe and did not understand. The two papers in this workshop illustrate the use of retroduction in qualitative social work research. We will have two respondents to this presentation. One is Johanna Barry from Loyola University of Chicago and a second from the audience. This person will be a volunteer.

1523648 What Do Women Want? Trauma-Informed Care in a Residential Opioid Addiction Recovery Program for Pregnant and Post-Partum Women. *Jonel Thaller (jthaller@bsu.edu) Ball State University, Jean Marie Place (jsplace@bsu.eduj) Ball State University, Kalyn Roessner (kmroessner@bsu.edu) Ball State University, and Greta Slater (gslater@bsu.edu) Ball State University*

Many women addicted to opioids have experienced extensive trauma in their lives. Though drug use may begin as self-medication, addiction can become yet another major life stressor that leads to further trauma. Gender-responsive, trauma-informed treatment acknowledges the burden that many women carry in meeting the societal expectations of selflessness and caring for others. Covington's (2008) approach to trauma-informed care provides a framework for women to interrogate/re-evaluate these relational expectations by 1) establishing personal safety (internally and externally), 2) remembering and mourning loss, then 3) reconnecting with one's self and others in a way that supports self-empowerment. We interviewed staff and clients (n=16) in a residential opioid addiction program attempting to institute a trauma-informed approach to learn more about how women's establishment of personal safety was supported or thwarted within the residential environment. Findings from this study illustrate what it means to staff and clients to engage in gender-responsive, trauma-informed treatment.

1522382 Research on Complex Topics Using Retroduction: Long-Term Life History Research: 33 Years and Counting. *Jane Gilgun (jgilgun@gmail.com), University of Minnesota*

My life history research with perpetrators of interpersonal violence began in 1985 and continues to this day. My initial framework was composes of feminist theories of what then was called sex role socialization and life course theory whose core concepts are power, privilege, and prestige. After several years, people asked when I would write my book. I said, "I don't know. I'm a slow learner." I was, indeed. Gradually, over decades, I have developed working theories that account for what has been hard for me to understand. Concepts such as redemptive violence—the belief that violence restores social order-- and toxic masculinity—are the most recent additions to my emerging theory. I will show how I use both deductive and inductive approaches to this long-term research.

Respondents: Johanna Barry, Loyola University of Chicago, and a volunteer

New Designs: Incorporating Qualitative Methods of the Evaluation of Services to Oppressed Populations
Chair: Thomas Kenemore, Loyola University
Union 405

Four panelists will discuss and explore the necessity of, and how to, incorporate the use of qualitative methods into evaluations of services provided to oppressed populations attended to by Social Work practitioners. Citizens returning from prison will serve as an example of an oppressed population that is, or should be, a primary focus of social work policy and practice. Panelists will review on-the-ground service delivery and how current evaluation methods do not capture the process of service delivery or relevant outcomes. We will show that program evaluations that are culturally responsive and transformative are essential to the task of understanding the change process and evaluating the effectiveness, from the viewpoint of the service user, of program services. Mixed-method designs will be proposed. Incorporation of qualitative approaches ensure that the voices of those served are central to the evaluation process.

The First Step Act and Qualitative Social Work Evaluation. *Brent In (bin1@luc.edu) Loyola University Chicago*

While the First Step Act now awaiting action in the US Senate appears to have potential benefits for sentencing and for people leaving prison, it also privileges quantitative methods and data as empirical evidence for determining what constitutes evidence-based practice and legitimate scientific inquiry. In this presentation, I will consider aspects of the bill that denigrates qualitative inquiry. The title of the bill is H.R.5682, First Step Act, 115th Congress (2017-2018). It passed in House and is now in the Senate.

Need for Exploratory Evidence for Reentry Program Evaluation. *Jo Cooper (Jo_Cooper@moep.uscourts.gov)Federal Probation Office Eastern District of Missouri,*

Governmental policies regarding service delivery to persons leaving prison and reentering society do not fit the realities of what actually is required. I will describe how service provision works on the ground and show how the federal government's evidence-based program requirements have affected service delivery and the experiences of persons reentering society. In addition, I will address issues regarding programs focused simply on the reduction of recidivism, when the real needs of this population may not center on desistance from crime and recidivism, but on providing supports such as job skills programs, housing, therapy and family life education. Most important, the goals and aspirations of the people undergoing reentry must be incorporated into service delivery.

Engaged Humility and Empowerment as Essential to a Program Evaluation Approach. *Leeane Kallemeyn (kallemeyn@luc.edc) Loyola University Chicago*

Effective program evaluations have clear philosophical, theoretical, and methodological rationales. I will discuss the need for engaged humility and empowerment, and I will explore the importance of evaluations that are culturally responsive and transformative. Within this framework, the viewpoints of service users are centered with the result that evaluators are positioned to understand change processes and outcomes. The results are evaluations with credibility, depth, and breadth.

Application of Qualitative Inquiry to Reentry Service Evaluation. *Thomas Kenemore (thomas@kenemore.org) Loyola University Chicago.*

Qualitative inquiry is important in the understanding of the experiences of returning citizens. I will illustrate the value of mixed-method approaches and complications that arise in the evaluation of reentry. Qualitative approaches ensure that the voices of those served are central to the evaluation protocol and will enable development of knowledge about the change process as it relates to service delivery.

1:00-2:20

Concurrent Sessions

Social Justice and Service User Perspectives
Chair: Rita Sørly, Norut Northern Research Institute
Union 314A

Social Justice as a Core Value in Global Social Work. *Dassi Postan-Aizik (hadassa.postan@ssw.umaryland.edu) Yezreel Valley College/University of Maryland, Corey Shdaimah (cshdaimah@ssw.umaryland.edu) University of Maryland, and Roni Strier (rstrier@univ.haifa.ac.il) University of Haifa*

The presentation will explore social justice as a core value for social workers around the world. Constructions and interpretations of social justice are greatly affected by different perspectives, contested positions, and unequal power dynamics. As societies become ever more diversified, and as socioeconomic divisions grow, the significance of social justice to practice may be questioned or lose its relevancy. We will present a qualitative study that draws on interviews and visual analysis with 16 American and 15 Israeli social work students who participated in a bi-national inter-professional seminar on social justice in divided cities. Findings suggest that social justice remains a core value, although it is both an organizing and disorganizing, unifying and dividing concept. We explore the contribution of positionality, a concept adopted from qualitative research, to social work practice and education to help gain a broader more critical awareness of social justice and navigate challenges in conflicted settings.

1490428 "I don't understand why I am treated this way." Stigmatization of Individuals with Disability: The Case of Ghana. *Magnus Mfoafo-M'Carthy (mmfoafomcarthy@wlu.ca) Wilfrid Laurier University, and Jeff Grischow (jgrischow@wlu.ca) Wilfrid Laurier University*

Challenges faced by persons with disabilities (PWIs) in Ghana are enormous due to prevailing cultural and societal practices that tend to stigmatize and socially exclude individuals with disability. Based on a study conducted in Kumasi, a city in Southern Ghana, this presentation examines challenges faced by individuals with disability and their caregivers. Using phenomenological methodology, the study explores the lived experience of participants based on their day-to-day realities. The participants' experience gives insight into challenges faced by individuals with disability and their family members. The intent of this study was not necessarily to generalize but rather to make a case for the majority of PWIs in Ghana. The study shows that stigma continues to dominate the discourse of PWIs in most countries in the sub-Saharan region of Africa. This trend could be a result of governments' unwillingness to invest the much-needed resources including human and social capital into these areas.

1528438 **"The Curse We Live With:" Earning a Living After Leprosy.** *Cynthia Sottie (csottie@gmail.com) Booth University College and Judith Kafui Darkey (judithdarkey@yahoo.com) Department of Social Welfare, Ministry of Gender, Children and Social Protection, Accra, Ghana*

In many parts of the developing world, illnesses that affect a person's physical appearance or mental functioning are highly stigmatized. The belief that such illnesses result from curses evokes fear. This study presents the lived-experiences of persons cured of leprosy on the challenges of earning a living given that they are often marginalised and isolated from mainstream society. Qualitative interviews were conducted with 20 participants from a leprosy colony in Ghana. Findings indicate that many lost their jobs due to leprosy and have limited opportunities to earn income. Some resorted to selling produce which often got rotten because no one would purchase from them. The study recommends educating communities to address stigma, enhancing capacities of persons cured of leprosy to engage in a variety of economic ventures and assisting them with finding markets.

1526489 **In the Dragon's Mouth: A Digital Performance Art Installation Exploring Mental Illness-Related Stigma in Trinidad** *Tracie. Rogers (tracie_rogers@usc.edu.tt) University of the Southern Caribbean and Jason Hunte (jmwhunte@gmail.com) Independent Consultant*

This study generated contextualized knowledge about living with mental illness by exploring experiences of internalized and social stigma in Trinidad. Five participants, diagnosed with mood and anxieties disorders, engaged as co-researchers to generate visual and textual data on their experiences of stigma. We used photovoice and crystallization as methodological strategies to produce coherent and nuanced analyses. We engaged multiple ways of examining data through thematic analysis and visual iconography. This paper will focus on the digital exhibition/performance installation that we used for disseminating study findings. While producing symbolic and context driven depictions of experiences with mental illness, In the Dragon's Mouth, used a dissemination strategy co-constructed with participants to provide opportunities for unprecedented critical dialogues with members of the public. In this paper, I examine the use of photography and performance as a dissemination strategy and discuss how the audience explored the social realities and support needs of people living with mental illness.

1471967 **Entering a New Landscape: User Invovlvement in Sami Perspectives and Contexts.** *Rita Sørly (rita.sorly@norut.no)* Norut Northern Research Institute *and Vår Mathisen (var.mathisen@uit.no)* Arctic University of Norway

The project deals with user involvement in Sami perspectives and context in Norwegian mental health services. The dominant Norwegian culture is expressed through social institutions and the health care system, and regulates what sorts of problems and what kind of social or cultural differences that are worth attention. There is little research-based knowledge about how user involvement can be understood and implemented in a Sami mental health context.

Qualitative Research that Begins with Conceptual Frameworks
Chair: Kelly Gross State University of New York at Albany
Union 314B

1490905 Testing and Tainting the Waters: LGBTQ Adult Grandchildren and Experiences Coming Out to Grandparents. *Sarah Reta Young (syoung@binghamton.edu) Binghamton University, Freda Coleman-Reed (fvcolemanreed@una.edu) University of North Alabama, and Debra Nelson-Gardell (dnelsong@sw.ua.edu) University of Alabama*

This study explores the relationships between lesbian, gay, bisexual, transgender, and queer (LGBTQ) adult grandchildren and their family members with a particular focus on grandparental relationships during the coming out process for the LGBTQ grandchild. To date, we have interviewed 10 LGBTQ adult grandchildren using a semi-structured interview protocol with recruitment continuing. Using the lens of family systems theory, we used open and thematic coding and found that: 1) Other family members frequently erect barriers (such as warnings that grandparents wouldn't be understanding) to prevent the grandchild from coming out to the grandparent(s). This often conflicted with how the grandchild's expected response from grandparents, and 2) When some participants "tested the waters," grandparent responses were identified as important to coming out. Based on this initial analysis, we argue that grandparents seem to be significant in the coming out process despite literature overwhelmingly focusing on parents.

1490804 Resilience Among Puerto Rican Families Post-Hurricane Maria. *Pilar Horner (phorner@msu.edu), Daniel Velez Ortiz (velezda@msu.edu) Michigan State University, Mikiko Sato (satomik1@msu.edu) Michigan State University, and Abbie Rebekah Nelson (nelso777@msu.edu) Michigan State University*

Family resilience in the face of catastrophic events offers new pathways for addressing familial outcomes; however little work has shown how Latino family resilience affects familial outcomes. Working in Florida, this study uses Walsh's family resilience framework (2016) and disaster resilience frameworks by Ososky & Osofsy (2017), to examine how Latino families post-Hurricane offer new insights for resilience theory. We used a multi-family art-based inquiry method coupled with multi-family focus groups. We worked with three different families from three different geographical areas in the greater Orlando, FL area for a total of nine focus groups. All work was conducted in Spanish. Focus groups revealed confirmatory evidence of Walsh's (2016) framework as well as new dimensions unique to Latino families. Latino family resilience contributes and expands to the current knowledge base after catastrophic events. Such information can improve social service delivery, policy applications, and theory generation.

1527229 Informal Networks and Use in Development: Changing the Face of Economics to Include the Social. *Kelly Gross (kgross@albany.edu) State University of New York at Albany*

Inquiry around small, informal networks for economic and community development is overlooked. Instead, the focus is on economic growth and development as the end game, without considering the intricate processes—such as informal networks--that are involved in development. However, small business owners depend on their social networks to be successful. Of growing importance, "business model intimacy," suggests that constructing shared identity and vision between a business and a community is key for sustainable community development (Simanis, & Hart, 2009). An inductive qualitative approach of a multi-case study explored informal networks as a component to development. Findings included informal networks being of importance, descriptors of types of networks, and how intricate to economics these networks could be. Implications include building research to inform experts to make development more inclusive and sustainable.

Autoethnography
Chair: Molly C. Driessen, University of Minnesota.
Union 404

1490172 Finding Lost Authoethnographic Voice: Considering Method Obstacles in Social Work. *Heather M Sloane (heather.sloane@utoledo.edu), University of Toledo*

In this paper the author will share excerpts from three unfinished autoethnographies. Observations will be shared about caregiving, micro aggression, and sexual fluidity and how progress on these works have been enhanced or hindered throughout the Ph.D. and tenure process. The author will discuss openly her fear of publishing such personal experiences as she pursued tenure in an environment unfamiliar with autoethnographic method. The author will also reflect back on autoethnography that occurred during the nurturing of a Ph.D. program and consider ways to create an environment open to autoethnography for interested students in undergraduate/graduate social work programs.

1520337 Women in the Wild: Writing Evocative Autoethnographies on Trauma, Nature, and Healing. *Cynthia Edmonds-Cady (cedmond@ilstu.edu) Illinois State University.*

This paper explores evocative autoethnography as a methodological approach, presenting a narrative on the healing power of wilderness and the natural environment. One woman's experience living with a violent, abusive partner is discussed, and how nature both empowered and healed her. Emphasis is on the writing process itself, and how the use of key fissures in the narrative helped

19

connect themes of gender, class, violence, motherhood, nature, and healing to present larger patterns that may resonate with trauma survivors. The purpose of this research is to evoke a response in readers, particularly those who either work with, or are themselves victims of violence. Attention is paid to the use of this methodological approach in connecting survivors to the healing potential of the natural environment. Possibilities for the use of this approach in therapeutic workshops for trauma survivors will be discussed, as well as its use as a participatory research method.

1489719 Meaning Making from Trauma: The Storied Self in Social Work Qualitative Inquiry. *Molly C. Driessen (dries032@umn.edu) University of Minnesota.*

The process of storying experiences of sexual violence significantly impacts the healing process for individuals creating meaning from their experiences. Critical qualitative inquiry, including writing as method, is needed within the field of social work to capture the complexities of sexual violence, provide space for the voices of victim-survivors, and identify contextual information that quantitative and traditional forms of inquiry cannot obtain. In creatively applying writing as method through combining formal academic writing, poetry, and story-telling, I practice vulnerability in this paper to convey the connection of my trauma within my research, education, and work. I am explicit in identifying how my past has shaped where I am today as well as where the current research needs are within the field of social work. Future research needs to include the voices of victim-survivors in creative, critical qualitative methods that explore how victim-survivors make meaning of their sexual violence.

2:30-3:50

Concurrent Sessions

Panel: Participatory Methods for Social Change
Chair: Candace Christensen, University of Texas, San Antonio
Union 314A

1487619 Facilitators and Barriers Faced by Early-Career Social Work Scholars Using Participatory Action Research. *Darren Cosgrove (dcosgrove@albany.edu), and Catherine Kramer (ckramer@albany.edu) University of Albany*

Social work researchers and practitioners face increasingly complex social challenges that demand practice-engaged research and research-engaged practice. Participatory action research (PAR) and community-based participatory research (CBPR) offer unique opportunities to span the boundaries that often exists between research and practice communities. Additionally, some social work researchers suggest that the values underpinning PAR/CBPR align with the values and ethics of the social work profession (e.g. social justice, self-determination and empowerment). Nevertheless, such methodologies are not widely represented in social work research literature or at professional conferences. The session will present the findings of a phenomenological study that collected data at ICQI 2018 and examined the experiences of early career social work scholars. Particular emphasis will be paid to the factors that acted as facilitators or barriers to participants' pursuit of PAR/CBPR. We will offer recommendations for developing supportive environments for this research to occur.

Shared Knowledge and Discourse: Changing the Privilege and Expertise Landscape. Kelly Gross (kgross@albany.edu) State *University of New York at Albany*

Oriented within Freire's *Pedagogy of the Oppressed* (1970), the presentation considers how researchers and "expert Westerners" must create shared knowledge systems with those who have differential experiences of power, privilege, and oppression. As researchers we forget that these rich, diverse knowledge systems exist and how their use is needed to interrupt continued colonialism and oppression. Using CBPAR methods allowed for the interruption of professional development by "expert" Westerners to indigenous teaching staff in Malawi, Africa. To right power and expertise imbalance, co- researchers from South Africa, Malawi, and the US created a dialogue about resilience, trauma, and traditional and indigenous ways of knowing. In the course of research, US and South African researchers who had been situated as "experts", reflected on their positionality and corresponding privilege, resulting in a righting of co-creation of knowledge to include a dialogic and critical feminist praxis for professional development (Nagar & Swarr, 2010).

1458063 **The Northern Norwegian Network for Participatory Research in the Field of Substance Abuse and Mental Health.** *Rita Sørly (rita.sorly@norut.no) NORUT Northern Research Institute*

It is a policy requirement in Norwegian health research that persons with own experience should contribute to research. Participatory research is a strategic effort to promote user perspectives in future health and care services. "The northern Norwegian network for participatory research in the field of substance abuse and mental health" was established in 2018, and the specific objectives of the network are to contribute to, participate in and support health and interdisciplinary research projects that promote user involvement, user management and user competence to develop methodological, practical and ethical competence in user-focused, practical and action oriented research and development work to stimulate user involvement in research and contribute to research-based education with a focus on user involvement to develop and maintain knowledge dialogues between users, researchers, practice fields and key actors. In this presentation we will give our thoughts and reflections, looking back at the first year as a network

1490968 **Engaging MSW Students in Implementing and Evaluating Photovoice to Transform Campus Rape Culture.** *Candace Christensen (candace.christensen@utsa.edu), University of Texas San Antonio, Inci Yilmazli Trout (yilmazli@uiwtx.edu) University of the Incarnate Word, and Beatrix Perez (beafloresperez@gmail.com) San Antonio College*

The research question guiding this study is: How does implementing and evaluating a photovoice project, focused on transforming campus rape culture, impact the Masters of Social Work (MSW) students who implemented and evaluated the project? The design of this study engages a constructivist paradigm. The data artifacts include 55 reflection papers generated by MSW students in a community practice course. The research team used grounded theory data analysis methods. We used line-by-line descriptive and analytic coding techniques as described by Charmaz (2014). Preliminary data analysis revealed the emergence of three categories: a) creating space for multiple perspectives, b) embracing the problem, c) critiquing how to engage the community. These preliminary findings portray how involving MSW students in this project supported students in valuing multiple perspectives, taking action on a given social issue, and encouraged critical thinking about how to engage the community in addressing sexual violence.

The Many Variations of Ethnographic Research
Chair: Vanessa Jara (vanedk@gmail.com) Universidad de Tarapacà
Union 314B

1490882 **A Cross-Examination of Patient-Centered Care**. *Kang Sun (kangsunbg@gmail.com) Kang Sun, University of Illinois*

Patient-Centered Care (PCC) foregrounds patients' needs as the focal point for healthcare professionals. However, the ways in which patients and their close social circle members make meanings of the healthcare services provided to them are understudied. Thus, the PCC model's potential strength is seriously undermined by such a gap in knowledge. This paper examines the potentials and limitations of PCC through a crossfire of social constitutionism and constitutivism in the context of an ethnographic study on post-stroke family care.

1491072 **Understanding the Perceptions of Low-Income Working Mothers in Rural Areas: Exploratory Analysis of Relative Care**. *Hyejoon Park (hyejoon.park@pittstate.edu) Pittsburg State University*

Formal and childcare arrangements (relative care), have a significant impact on the economic and social conditions of low-income families. However as opposed to formal childcare, there is a dearth of study to understand the families utilizing relatives for childcare and its impact of relative care to those families. This study used the extended ethnographic comparative case method and grounded theory to analyze in-depth interviews of nine low-income working mothers selected by purposive and snowball sampling, living in a mid-Western rural area—five Whites, two African Americans, and two Hispanic/Latina mothers with school-aged children. Participants did not receive public assistance for relative care. Findings show agreement that relative care contributed to their emotional/psychological well-being. They chose relative care for safety and felt comfortable knowing that caregivers are someone that they know. In addition, all Hispanic mothers mentioned that it is family responsibility to take care of their children.

1490981 **Fieldwork and Outreach to Invisible Migrant Farmworkers in Michigan.** Ken Saldanha (ksaldanh@emich.edu) Eastern Michigan University

Migrant farmworkers contribute to food systems and the local economy. However, they are rendered invisible in historical accounts and tourist narratives. Local residents are also unaware of their presence, even though they continue to arrive each successive year in the local area and stay through the entire agricultural season. This presentation highlights migrant farmworkers in a few counties in western Michigan. Through fieldwork, outreach, fieldnotes, and autoethnographic accounts, descriptions of labor camps, farmworkers, H-2A workers, and their housing and living conditions will be highlighted. The presentation will portray how farmworkers are able to maintain a singular focus on work, and despite uncertain and isolating conditions on multiple fronts, they continue to work diligently, providing for themselves and their families. The importance of 'outreach' and its accompanying nuances in establishing contact and delivering services to farmworkers and their families will also be discussed.

1518212 **The Ethnographic Tradition Within Social Work Curricula and Practices in Chilean Universities.** Vanessa Jara (vanedk@gmail.com) Universidad de Tarapacá and Cesar Cisneros (cesar.cisneros@pucv.cl) QualAnalytics, Chile

From its origins, ethnography was conceived as a method of knowledge production. The twentieth century can testify their adoption by different disciplines. We must be critical in the analysis of the use of this method, mixed and multiple par excellence, since its massive diffusion can lead to lack of rigor and lack of systematicity during research. Through documentary research, a conceptual analysis is conducted with special emphasis on topics, approaches and data production techniques. We propose a critical analysis of some current ethnographical practices. The paper is criticizing the current stage of teaching qualitative methods in Chilean social work schools. This paper claims for a creative performance of ethnography at levels of teaching and practicing to educate the future social workers our democratic societies would look for it.

Puzzles and Challenges in Social Work Qualitative Inquiry
Chair: Richard Weaver (rdweav03@louisville.edu) University of Louisville
Union 404

1490084 **Understanding Recruitment and Implementation for the Illinois Youth Survey: A Qualitative Approach.** Kelly L Clary (valenck2@illinois.edu), Hyun Jung Kim (hjk3@illinois.edu), Crystal Reinhart (reinhrt@illinois.edu), and Douglas C Smith (smithdc@illinois.edu)

Epidemiological surveys implemented within schools are important so systems can effectively create prevention and intervention programs to positively alter youths' health behaviors by representative trend data. However, there are many barriers to recruiting sites in such studies. Through semi-structured qualitative interviews this study uncovered 30 key informants' challenges when deciding to implement the Illinois Youth Survey (IYS). A descriptive and interpretive analysis approach investigated, participants' thoughts on improving future recruitment procedures. The most prominent barriers were the timing of the study and utilization of data. The most common suggestions to improve recruitment include creating a contextualized approach through communication and providing concrete examples of how data can be applied. Findings will improve future recruitment procedures for others who have similar challenges. If schools, counties, and states have representative data they can ethically tailor their programming to meet the needs of their population.

1520015 Experiences of Adult Foster Care Providers Across Two States: Valuing and Supporting Opportunities for Reciprocity. *Kelly Munly (kam6832@psu.edu) Penn State Altoona*

We explored Adult Foster Care (AFC) as an option for community-based long-term care across two states, North Carolina and Pennsylvania. Although this option varies greatly in structure and accessibility among states, AFC settings are licensed by each state and typically provide service for 2-6 residents per home. Semi-structured interviews were conducted with providers to understand their experiences with AFC operations and their relationships with residents. A most salient code that emerged from the data analysis related to reciprocity between residents and providers. Recognizing the value of reciprocity has implications for enhancing provider-resident experiences. Acknowledging the value of resident contributions to provider experience is one step further toward facilitating resident inclusion in communities. Providers who feel that their lives are improved by residents' reciprocity may also find it more feasible to sustain their demanding care and administrative roles, contributing to one of the more cost-effective and community-integrated options for long-term care.

Latino Elders' Perceptions on Positive Aging. *Wendy Wan-Jung Hsieh (wjhsieh2@illinois.edu) University of Illinois at Urbana-Champaign*

Older Latinos are a rapidly growing segment of the older adult population in the United States. Yet studies have overlooked how Latino older adults conceptualize "aging well," "positively," or "successfully." To address the cross-cultural differences in conceptualizations between older Latinos from diverse national, ethnic, linguistic, and socio-economic backgrounds, we conducted nine focus groups with Latino participants ages 55 and older (N = 101) in Cook County, Illinois. Participants were asked to brainstorm and discuss what thoughts phrases like, "positive aging" or "successful aging" or "aging well," bring to mind. Six audio-recorded focus groups were conducted in Spanish and three in English. We wrote down statements during the focus groups and from listening to the audio-recordings. With the assistance of Latino community leaders and from the PALS (Positive Aging for Latinos Study) Steering Committee (N = 20), we used the concept mapping to construct 85 statements from the participants in the focus groups. Findings will be used as springboard for future research and will be used as recommendations to services providers to develop culturally tailored interventions and programs for Latino seniors to promote positive aging.

1490834 **The Impacts of Lived Experience as a Youth in the Child Welfare System on Direct Care Staff in Residential Treatment Centers.** *Lisa Purdy (lisa.purdy@louisville.edu), Sara Williams (saram.williams@louisville.edu) University of Louisville, Jill Randall (jill.randall@louisville.edu) University of Louisville, and Lesley M. Harris (lesley.harris@louisville.edu) University of Louisville*

In residential treatment centers, direct care staff play a significant role in determining outcomes for youth. Little is known about the experience of direct care staff who were in "out of home care" as a youth: foster, residential, or kinship care, or care by fictive kin. This study aims to explore and describe their experience. We conducted in-depth qualitative interviews with direct care staff in Kentucky with lived experience as a youth in out of home care. Grounded theory techniques were used to analyze the interviews. Having lived experience affected the staffs' approach to their role through the simultaneous management of past trauma and present conflict with children in their care. Their professional relationships were also affected; staff saw themselves as "other," balancing stigma and status through their unique position. We will provide recommendations for the hiring process, training, and supervision of these direct care staff.

1490844 **Conflicts of Athletic Identity: Examining Female Athletic Identity and Developmental Transitions.** *Richard Weaver (rdweav03@louisville.edu) University of Louisville*

Currently in the United States, there are more than 250,000 intercollegiate female athletes. However, there is limited research on female athletic identity and the impact of significant developmental transitions. This study evaluated athletic identity and how it positively and negatively affected periods of developmental transition. I used a phenomenological approach and conducted in-depth interviews with 15 current intercollegiate female athletes at four-year academic institutions. I used grounded theory techniques were used to analyze the transcripts. I found that parents played a major role in the development of athletic identity by encouraging athletic participation as early as five years old. Strong athletic identity was created through Sports as a year-round activity with school, recreational, and travel teams created a strong athletic identity. Identity conflicts emerged during transition periods and when new experiences and expectations were introduced. I will make recommendations for interventions and services that buffer stress and increase wellness for female student-athletes.

4:00-5:20	Illini Room A

Plenary Session

Town Hall Meeting
Reflections on Social Work Day and What's Next
Chair: Jane F. Gilgun, University of Minnesota

5:30-6:30	Illini Room A

Tea & Coffee Reception Illini Union

A Chance to Mingle
All are Welcome

Midwest Barbeque

Qualitative Inquiry in Social Work

Qualitative Inquiry in Social Work is a newsletter of Social Work Day. The first two issues are available on free on ResearchGate and for $.99 on Amazon. The newsletter is a global publication that bridges gaps between oral transmission and journal articles. The writing is informal, personal, and interesting and will match our experiences as qualitative inquirers.

Qualitative inquiry includes reflections, speculations, theorizing, and creating accounts not only of human phenomena but also how our efforts might bring about positive social change. See the articles in the first two issues for an idea of what I mean.

Please consider writing for *QISW*. The writing is informal, first person, and compelling. Authors have shared some of their deepest experiences in ways that show courage, resistance, and desire for positive social change. We are accepting submissions for the third issue now. The deadline is 1 July 2019.

A regular feature is *What's Going on in Your Home Regions*. We'd love to hear from people throughout the world. There's so much going on that has a place for qualitative inquiry. will have a special section on What's Going on in Your Home Regions.

Another feature is *Ask Dr. Debra*, where researchers pose dilemmas they encounter in their work, and Debra Nelson-Gardell, University of Alabama, USA, responds. A recent question is how do I know informants are telling the truth?

The first and second issues of *Qualitative Inquiry in Social Work* is now available free on ResearchGate. The best informal writing in social work inquiry is in this enhanced newsletter. Link to first issue:
https://www.researchgate.net/publication/327117935_Qualitative_Inquiry_in_Social_Work_Global_Perspectives_11

Link to second issue:
https://www.researchgate.net/publication/332497436_Qualitative_Inquiry_in_Social_Work_21_January_2019